WHAT COLOR IS MY WORLD?

THE LOST HISTORY OF AFRICAN-AMERICAN INVENTORS

First edition in this format 2013

The Library of Congress has cataloged the hardcover edition as follows:

Abdul-Jabbar, Kareem, date.
What color is my world? : the lost history of African-American inventors /
by Kareem Abdul-Jabbar and Raymond Obstfeld. — 1st ed.
p.   cm.
Summary: While twins Ella and Herbie help the handyman Mr. Mital work
on their new home, he tells them about such inventors as Granville Woods,
Dr. Henry T. Sampson, and James West, giving them a new view of their
heritage as African Americans.
ISBN 978-0-7636-4564-9 (hardcover)
[1. Inventors—Fiction. 2. African Americans—Fiction. 3. Moving,
Household—Fiction. 4. Brothers and sisters—Fiction. 5. Twins—
Fiction.]   I. Obstfeld, Raymond, date. II. Title.
PZ7.A1589337Wh 2012
[Fic]—dc23   2011018610

ISBN 978-0-7636-6442-8 (paperback)

16 17 18 BVG 10 9 8 7 6 5 4

Printed in Berryville, VA, U.S.A.

This book was typeset in Plantin and Novarese.

Candlewick Press
99 Dover Street
Somerville, Massachusetts 02144

visit us at www.candlewick.com

WHAT COLOR IS MY WORLD?

THE LOST HISTORY OF AFRICAN-AMERICAN INVENTORS

KAREEM ABDUL-JABBAR

& RAYMOND OBSTFELD

illustrated by **BEN BOOS** & **A. G. FORD**

CANDLEWICK PRESS

TABLE OF CONTENTS

« 1 »

"You've got to use your imagination," Mama encouraged us.

That's what adults always say when something looks really awful but they want you to say something nice anyway.

Mama smiled weakly and waited for us to say something nice.

And waited.

More waiting.

Finally, my twin sister, Ella, shook her head. "My imagination must be low on batteries, because all I can see is some creepy old house out of some horror movie."

"Thank you, Ella." Mama frowned. Then she turned to me. "What do you think, Herbie?"

"It's great, Mama. Very, uh, roomy."

Ella stood behind Mama and made an exaggerated kissing face at me. But the truth was, I kind of liked the old place. I stomped my foot on the wooden porch. "Solid," I said, and Mama smiled.

"Herrrrrbieeee," Ella sang, "I am the Ghost of Losers Past. We welcome you to our ranks."

Mama ignored Ella and gestured at the house. "It's got three bedrooms upstairs, so you'll each have your own room. That'll be a nice change, huh?"

Ella actually perked up at that. "I won't have to smell his skanky socks after basketball practice."

"And I won't have to listen to your dumb phone calls."

"Knock, knock," a voice said from behind us.

Mama turned and smiled. "Roger! You're early!"

"We've got a lot of work ahead of us, ma'am."

"That's the truth," Mama said. "You have the list of what I need to pick up?"

"Right here." He pulled out a long, handwritten list from the top pocket of his bib overalls and handed it to Mama.

"Kids, this is Mr. Mital. He's a handyman Dad and I met at church."

"Roger Edward Mital," he said, offering his hand. We shook it and told him our names. His hand was rough and callused. Like Dad's. Even though Dad worked as an executive in a bank with a big metal desk and an assistant and wore suits and ties and shiny shoes, he still liked to work with his hands on weekends.

"You two will help Mr. Mital while I go get more supplies." She whistled at the list. "A *lot* of supplies."

"It'll all be worth it," Mr. Mital said. "You'll see."

Mom nodded, still staring at the long list. "Walk me to the car," she told Ella and me.

When we got to the car, she said, "You do what Mr. Mital says, you hear me? We are lucky to have him."

Ella patted Mama's shoulder. "Relax, Mama."

Mama locked eyes with Ella. "I mean it, girl."

When Mama's car was out of sight, we turned toward the house and there was Mr. Mital.

"I take it you two are less than thrilled with your new home." Mr. Mital had a well-worn hammer in the loop of his overalls. He smelled like the peppermint tea Mama always drinks when she gets home from work. She's a middle-school principal (not at the school Ella and I go to, thank goodness!).

"We were hoping for something . . . newer," Ella said. "Like the Covent Gardens homes they're building over on Draper Street. They have a community pool."

"And a hot tub," I added. "And tennis courts."

"New isn't necessarily better," Mr. Mital said. "If you look closely at this place, you'll see some exquisite craftsmanship." We walked into the house.

"But you won't see a pool," Ella said.

Mr. Mital laughed. "Nope. But you'll see something else."

"Hepatitis?"

"History. Many people worked across the centuries to make a house like this. This house is the culmination of all human progress."

"Sounds crowded," Ella said with a snort.

"Sounds like a museum," I said.

"Oh, it is." Mr. Mital nodded. "A museum is a celebration of achievement. Your parents' achievement in providing a home for their family, but also a celebration of the history of humankind, the history of America, and the history of African Americans."

Ella laughed. "African Americans? Unless this was a station on the Underground Railroad, I don't see any African-American history." She cupped her hands and shouted up the stairs, "Dr. King, are you up there watching MTV with Harriet Tubman?"

"Ella," I said, nudging her, "knock it off."

"There's more to our history than slavery, jazz, sports, and civil rights marches."

"We know that," Ella said, getting sore.

"Do you know a lot of African-American scientists?" Mr. Mital asked.

Ella looked at me.

"C'mon, genius," Ella whispered to me. "Name some black scientists."

I'm sure I'd read about a few, but I couldn't remember a lot of names. Finally, I said, "George Washington Carver."

"The peanut guy," Ella said with a triumphant look.

"Amazing man," Mr. Mital agreed. "They called him the 'Black Leonardo,' after Leonardo da Vinci. Who else you got on that list?"

Ella and I looked at each other. Then we shrugged.

Mr. Mital walked over to the wall and flipped the light switch. Overhead, a bare lightbulb burst ablaze with light.

"Who invented the lightbulb?" he asked.

"Thomas Edison," I said.

"You going to tell us he was black?" Ella said.

"It was a trick question," Mr. Mital said. "No one invented the lightbulb."

"What?" Ella and I said at the same time.

"Oh, Edison had a lot to do with bringing us the lightbulb. But no one invents anything. Not by themselves."

"Then how come all the history books are filled with names of inventors?" I asked.

"It's easier for people to remember one name. And easier for teachers to test you on those names. In truth, all inventors only improve on what's come before them. They should be called innovators rather than inventors. See, inventing is like standing in a bucket brigade. People stand in a line that stretches from a water source to a fire, and they pass buckets of water up the line. The last person in line throws the water on the fire and gets all the credit for putting out the fire. Inventors are like the people in that line, each one contributing, but the one who throws the water gets the credit as the inventor."

I pulled out the blank journal tucked into my back pocket and started scribbling what he said. I even drew a bucket brigade. My whole life is in my journals. I have more than four hundred of them, all stacked neatly in my bookcase in chronological order from the time I was five.

"Sir Isaac Newton once said—"

"The apple-proves-gravity guy," Ella said.

"Right. He said, 'If I have seen farther than others, it is by standing on the shoulders of giants.' Meaning that whatever he achieved is because of what he learned from all the great scientists that came before him."

"So, what does the lightbulb have to do with African Americans?" Ella asked. The edge had gone from her voice.

Mr. Mital grinned. "Ever heard of Lewis Latimer?"

We shook our heads.

"Let me ask you this: what color is electricity?" He flicked the lightbulb on and off.

I thought for a second. "White?"

"It's yellow," Ella scoffed.

"Lightning looks white when it flashes," I reminded her.

"Yeah? Well, I don't think that—"

"This electricity," Mr. Mital interrupted, "is black."

"Black?" Ella and I said at the same time. We both stared at the lightbulb.

"You sure your glasses just aren't dirty?" Ella said.

"This city gets its electricity from the nuclear power plant. In fact, twenty percent of all the electricity in the U.S. comes from nuclear energy. That is thanks to Dr. Henry T. Sampson, who invented the gamma electric cell, which makes it possible to convert nuclear radiation into electricity."

Ella looked at me. "How come you didn't know that, Thomas Nerdison?"

I shrugged. Good question. Why didn't I?

"Speaking of Thomas Edison," Mr. Mital said, "you ever hear of Granville T. Woods?"

Ella and I shook our heads.

"He was known as the 'Black Thomas Edison' because of all his inventions. In fact, Edison even tried to hire Woods. Alexander Graham Bell's company bought Woods's 'telegraphony' invention." Mr. Mital flicked the light switch off and on again. "Black electricity."

"Black electricity." Ella chuckled. She grabbed my journal out of my hands and started scribbling notes.

"You are going to love this next part," Mr. Mital said. He leaned forward as if he was about to tell us a deep, dark secret.

Ella and I leaned forward, too, listening.

He picked up a broom in each hand and tossed them to us. "Get to work."

He walked out of the room, but we could hear his laughter echoing in the hallway.

As soon as he was gone, I grabbed my journal back from Ella and started writing down everything he'd told us.

"You're crazy if you think I'm doing all the sweeping while you scribble away," Ella said.

"I don't want to forget what he said. I want to find out more later."

She snorted and started sweeping, then stopped and snapped her fingers at me. "Give me some paper, too. Just to make sure you get it right."

DR. HENRY T. SAMPSON
(born 1934)
Gamma Electric Cell

ELLA'S FAST FACTS:

* There are 442 nuclear-power reactors in the world.

* 104 of them are in the United States.

* These reactors provide 14 percent of the world's electricity and 20 percent of the U.S.'s energy.

DR. HENRY T. SAMPSON is just as much an action hero as the muscle-bound Samson from the Bible. Born in Mississippi in 1934, Dr. Sampson was the first African American to earn a PhD in nuclear engineering, which he did in 1967. In 1971, he invented something called the gamma electric cell, which converts radiation directly into electricity. It was a big deal and Dr. Sampson won a bunch of awards for his invention. Here's something interesting about him that has nothing to do with science: he also wrote books and produced documentary films about overlooked African-American filmmakers of the nineteenth and twentieth centuries.

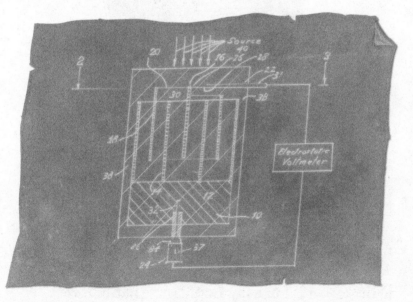

GRANViLLE T. WOODS
(1856–1910)
Induction Telegraph

ELLA'S FAST FACTS:

* In 1890, there were 163,597 miles of railroad track in the U.S.

* Abraham Lincoln signed the Pacific Railway Act on July 1, 1862, which paved the way for the Transcontinental Railroad and led to many inventions that improved railroad safety.

When GRANVILLE T. WOODS was ten, he quit school
because his family needed the money. He worked in a machine
shop that repaired railroad equipment and went nuts
over all the electrical machines. He paid guys that worked
there to teach him how everything worked. Eventually,
he attended college and studied engineering. He invented
stuff like a steam-boiler furnace for trains, improved the
telephone transmitter so the sound was clearer, and even
improved the egg incubator. In 1887, he patented his most
famous invention: the induction telegraph. The induction
telegraph allowed moving trains to send and receive messages
from railroad stations, making train travel a lot safer.
Thomas Edison was so impressed that he offered Woods a
job, but the "Black Edison" (that's what they called him)
preferred to stay the one and only Black Granville Woods
and continued to work for himself.

Lewis Howard Latimer
BRIGHT IDEAS

SON OF SLAVES

Lewis Howard Latimer was born on September 4, 1848, in Chelsea, Massachusetts, the youngest of four children. Just six years earlier, his parents, George and Rebecca Latimer, had been slaves in Virginia. Wanting their children to be born free from slavery, they fled from their owners to Boston, Massachusetts. Once they arrived in Boston, George was jailed as a fugitive slave while Rebecca hid and waited for him. Two prominent men championed George's release: Frederick Douglass, an influential ex-slave and the first African American to run for vice president, and William Lloyd Garrison, famed abolitionist and editor. Nevertheless, the judge ruled that George should be returned to his owner in Virginia. Fortunately, an African-American minister paid George's owner four hundred dollars (about $9,600 today) for George to be freed.

Lewis attended elementary school, where he excelled at reading and drawing. But, like most young men of that era, he spent most of his time working with his father at various jobs to support their family.

In 1864, with the Civil War at its bloodiest peak, sixteen-year-old Lewis joined the navy. After serving on the Union gunboat the USS *Massasoit*, he was honorably discharged in 1865.

LIGHTING UP LIFE

Latimer returned to Boston and landed a three-dollars-a-week job as an office boy at Crosby and Gould, a patent law firm that specialized in protecting inventors' patents. Here, Latimer observed the draftspeople creating their elaborate and precise drawings of clients' inventions and taught himself how to do the same thing. After practicing on his own for several months, Lewis asked the company for the chance to show what he could do. Surprising and impressing everyone at the company with his skill, Latimer was promoted to draftsperson at twenty dollars a week.

In 1876, Latimer was hired by Alexander Graham Bell, a teacher of deaf children, to draw his invention for a patent application. The invention was the telephone. Latimer and Bell worked all night to finish the blueprints and were able to file the patent just a few hours before another inventor working to patent a version of the telephone, making Bell the official inventor.

In 1880, Latimer moved to Brooklyn, New York, to work for inventor Hiram Maxim, the founder of the U.S. Electric Lighting Company and a rival to Thomas Edison. During this time, Latimer devised a method for enclosing the lightbulb filament in a cardboard envelope, which kept the filament from breaking. This made the bulb more efficient. Although he received a patent for this breakthrough, all profits went to Maxim.

In 1884, Latimer's expertise in electric lighting was so highly regarded that he was hired by Thomas Edison's company. Latimer helped Edison in three areas:

(1) navigating the tricky patent application process;

(2) protecting Edison's patents by investigating claims against Edison and testifying as an expert witness;

(3) amassing a comprehensive library on all available knowledge of incandescent lighting.

A few years later, Latimer wrote *Incandescent Electric Lighting: A Practical Description of the Edison System* (1890), which was the "bible" on incandescent lighting. Latimer continued to work for Edison and patent inventions for the next twenty-seven years. In 1911, Latimer went to work for a private consulting firm, until he retired in 1922. He continued to invent and teach until his death, in 1928.

Renaissance Family Man

Lewis Latimer was an important figure in the development of the lightbulb, but he loved the arts and had a passion for science. He painted portraits, played the flute, and wrote poetry, music, and plays.

His family life brought him great joy. He married Mary Wilson in 1873, and they had two daughters, Janette and Louise.

He was active in his Unitarian church and was an activist for civil rights. In his free time, he taught mechanical engineering, drawing, and English to immigrants. To honor his achievements, the Lewis H. Latimer School in Brooklyn was named after him in 1968. In 2006, Lewis Latimer was inducted into the National Inventors Hall of Fame.

DID EDISON INVENT
THE FIRST LIGHTBULB?

Historians list twenty-two inventors of incandescent lamps *before* Thomas Edison. In fact, Edison lost several patent lawsuits in which courts ruled that others, notably Joseph Swan in England and William Sawyer in the U.S., had invented lightbulbs before him.

Edison and his staff of ten scientists clearly used the work of Joseph Swan in particular when developing their own version of the lightbulb. Edison also bought the patents of other inventors. He and his team were able to vastly improve the lightbulb to burn longer and brighter than earlier versions and helped to make the technology less expensive.

Despite not being the original inventor of the lightbulb, Edison is responsible for making electricity easily available. He realized that in order for the lightbulb to become popular, an entire infrastructure of generators, wires, fixtures, and lamps would be necessary. Edison used his considerable reputation as an inventor to entice investors to give him large amounts of money needed to get this massive infrastructure built. His genius as a scientist — and as a businessman — helped to bring electricity to the average home.

« 2 »

About an hour later, Ella stopped sweeping and pulled out her cell phone. She started punching numbers.

I kept sweeping. "Who are you calling? Mama?"

"Pizza. I'm starving and they deliver."

"I don't have any money," I said. "Do you?"

"We'll let the Mad Hatter pay. A guy that smart should have some cash, right?"

Mr. Mital's voice startled us. "'Why is a raven like a writing desk?'"

Ella and I just stared at him.

"That's a little weird," Ella said.

Mr. Mital grinned. "If you're going to call me the Mad Hatter, you should at least know what he says in *Alice in Wonderland*."

"Does it make more sense in the book than when you say it?"

Mr. Mital picked up a crumpled brown paper bag from the huge pile of trash we had just swept together. He shook it open, walked over to Ella, and nodded for her to put the cell phone into the bag. Ella hesitated. I knew she was trying to figure out just what Mama's punishment would be for not doing as she was told. She must have come to the same conclusion I did—two weeks without her cell phone—because she dropped it into the bag. He walked over to me, and I dropped mine in, too.

He twisted the neck of the bag shut and briskly walked out of the room. "Follow me."

Ella and I exchanged looks, then followed him. We heard his rapid footsteps pattering down the stairs to the first floor. He moved fast for an older guy.

When Ella and I reached the bottom of the stairs, Mr. Mital was waiting for us, still clutching the paper bag with our phones.

"First things first," he said. He carried the bag to the carpenter's workbench, which was covered with tools. He set the bag down, picked up a hammer, and started slamming the hammer into the bag. Loud crunching could be heard with each strike.

Ella started screaming, "Are you crazy? I had to babysit for a year to buy that!"

She ran over and grabbed the bag, then opened it and stared. Then she reached in and pulled out a handful of bent nails, chunks of plaster, a couple broken mousetraps, and assorted other trash.

"Where are our phones?" Ella demanded.

"Safe," said Mr. Mital.

"How'd you do that?" I asked.

" 'Why is a raven like a writing desk?' "

Ella stared at Mr. Mital.

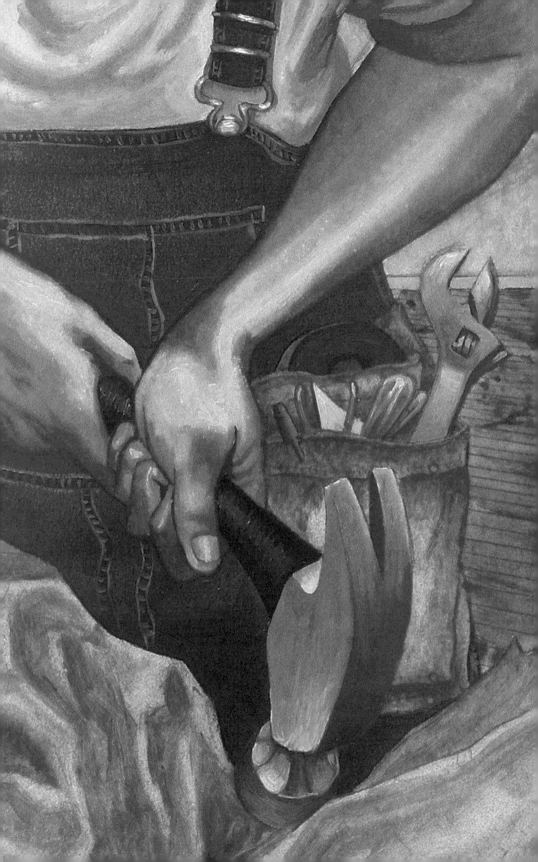

"Check your pockets," he said.

Ella reached into her pocket and pulled out her cell phone. Intact. I reached into my jeans and found mine there, too.

"H-how'd you do that?" Ella stammered.

"You see what you want to see," Mr. Mital said. "But the world is so much more."

"But that was some kind of voodoo magic or something," Ella said.

"Magic is just encouraging people to see things they haven't imagined yet. That's what inventors do. Isn't television magic? Isn't an airplane? How about turning mold into medicine?" He pointed at our cell phones. "When you look at those, what do you see?"

Ella and I looked at our phones.

"A phone," Ella said flatly.

"I see an African-American kid named James West who, at eight, was so curious about how things worked that he nearly electrocuted himself repairing a radio. He later invented the microphone that is inside your cell phone. I see another black inventor, Dr. Mark Dean, who took computers out of laboratories and into business offices and homes. Without him, you wouldn't have a computer in your home — or in your phone. And I see Dr. Valerie Thomas, whose invention that creates 3-D images may be the future of television, video games, and medical diagnosis. That's what I see."

Ella snorted.

I took out my journal. "James West, Mark Dean, and Valerie Thomas."

Ella made another loud kissing-up sound, but I hardly heard her over the sound of my pencil scratching across the paper.

DR. MARK DEAN
(born 1957)
Personal Computer Stuff

ELLA'S FAST FACTS:

* Dr. Dean is a vice president at IBM.

* He developed the color graphics adapter (which gave color to PC displays).

* He led the team that developed the world's first gigahertz microprocessor (right).

OK, I use a computer pretty much every day. But not like my brother, who uses it exclusively for schoolwork. (Which is what our parents told us is the only thing we could use it for.) I use it for school, too, but how else am I going to keep my Facebook profile up to date? And I sometimes get homework assignments and notes from my girlfriends. That should count, right? Whatever. The point is, until DR. MARK DEAN came along, computers were mostly giant boxes too big and clumsy to have in the average home or office. Then he and another scientist, Dennis Moeller, invented the Industry Standard Architecture (ISA) systems bus, which is the doohickey that allows you to connect external devices such as printers or keyboards. He made the computer practical for the rest of us. In fact, Dr. Dean holds three of the nine patents for the original IBM personal computer and holds more than forty patents in all.

He kind of reminds me of my brother: when Dr. Dean was a kid in Jefferson City, Tennessee, he got straight As, too. Must have been weird, though, when his classmates kept asking him if he was really black because he was so smart. No one asks my brother that, so I guess we've made some progress. Of course, they do ask him if he's from this planet because he's such a dork, but that's another story.

DR. VALERIE L. THOMAS
(born 1943)
Illusion Transmitter

ELLA'S FAST FACTS:

* The first 3-D movie shown to paying customers was in 1915!

* The audience wore red-and-green glasses that combined the two movie images, which had been shot 2½ inches apart.

* Back in the 1950s, most of the 3-D movies were horror films, so they could show knives and stuff poking out at the audience.

If there's one thing I've learned from listening to Mr. Mital's stories about all these amazing inventors, it's that most of them had a really hard time being taken seriously as scientists just because they were black. Now, imagine how much harder it was if you were black and a woman. First, you'd have to overcome the whole race thing ("Blacks aren't smart enough to compete with whites blah blah blah."). Then you'd also have to put up with a whole bunch of crap about being a girl ("Girls just aren't as smart as men yadda yadda yadda."). That's what makes DR. VALERIE L. THOMAS so cool. She worked her way up to associate chief of the Space Science Data Operations Office at the National Aeronautics and Space Administration (NASA), retiring in 1995.

In 1980, she received a patent for an "illusion transmitter," which creates three-dimensional projections. Many believe this is the future of television and video games. Thanks to Dr. Thomas, one day geeks everywhere will be romping through their World of Warcraft realms as if their Orcs were right in front of them. For the rest of us, doctors are also using her invention to create 3-D images of the body to better diagnose patients.

JAMES E. WEST
EVERY VOICE DESERVES TO BE HEARD

ALWAYS A FIXER

James Edward West was born in Farmville, Virginia, on February 10, 1931. Even as a young child, James loved to tinker. When he was eight years old, he tried to repair a broken radio. After "fixing" the radio, he stood on the brass footboard of his bed so he could plug the radio into the ceiling outlet. When he shoved the plug into the socket, 120 volts of electricity burst through his body. Luckily, his brother saw what was happening and shoved him to the floor, breaking the electrical current and saving James's life. That experience inspired James to explore the science of electricity even more.

Learning was not easy for James because he suffered from dyslexia, a learning disability that makes reading difficult. James memorized his textbooks in order to hide his problem from his teachers and friends. His dyslexia didn't prevent him from earning top grades and being accepted by one of the best schools in the country, Temple University, in 1953.

When he told his parents he was going to major in physics, they tried to talk him out of it. The only professional jobs open to a black man in the South then were teacher, preacher, doctor, or lawyer. Recalled James, "My father introduced me to three black men who had earned doctorates in chemistry and physics. The best jobs they could find were at the post office. My father said I was taking the long road toward working at the post office."

Giving People a Voice

While attending Temple University, West worked as a summer intern at Bell Laboratories, a major telephone company. When he graduated from Temple in 1957, Bell hired him on full-time as an acoustical scientist. At that time, the microphones that were used in telephones were expensive and required a large battery. So Bell assigned West and German-born physicist Gerhard M. Sessler to team up and create a compact microphone that was highly sensitive yet relatively inexpensive. In 1964, their collaboration resulted in patent number

3,118,022 for an electroacoustic transducer, also called a foil-electret microphone, which revolutionized the microphone and communication industries. The technology was even used on racetracks, where West's advances allowed drivers to communicate despite a lot of background noise.

West remained working at Bell Labs for forty years, amassing two hundred patents. In 2001, he accepted a position as research professor at Whiting School of Engineering at Johns Hopkins University.

A Father Figure to Many

James West has a wife and daughter, but his family is much bigger than that. At Bell Labs, West was a founding member of the Association of Black Laboratories Employees (ABLE), which encouraged management to fund programs that helped more than five hundred non-white students earn degrees in science, engineering, and mathematics.

The world has responded to West's dedication by honoring him many times over. Among his achievements, in 1995, New Jersey declared him Inventor of the Year; in 1999, he was inducted into the National Inventors Hall of Fame; and in 2006, President George W. Bush awarded him the National Medal of Technology.

As for what the future holds for Dr. James West, his mind is too active to slow down. "My hobby is my work," he says. "I have the best of both worlds because I love what I do. Do I ever get tired of it? Not so far."

MICROPHONES AND RACE-CAR DRIVERS

What do microphones have to do with being a successful race-car driver? During a Formula One race, a car can reach speeds of 225 miles per hour. Because the speed is so dangerous, the driver must stay in continuous contact with his or her pit crews and team managers to know when to come in for maintenance and what to be aware of on the track ahead. The problem is that the noise level inside the car is extremely loud. "The noise inside the race car is about the same as a 747 jet if you're 300 feet away," explained Dr. James E. West. "That lies just under the threshold of pain." Drivers would have to wait to talk until they were forced to slow down for difficult corners. Because driving through those corners takes so much concentration, it wasn't the best time to try to hold a serious conversation. But Dr. West and his team were able to cut the background noise in half by using several microphones, microprocessors to track sound, and software that filters background sounds. Now drivers can focus on pushing their cars to even greater speeds, without sacrificing their own safety.

"You don't think that was weird?" Ella said as she dragged her soapy sponge across the window.

"What?"

She stared at me as if I had just tried to put my pants on over my head. "Are you kidding me, Dorkenstein? The whole reappearing cell phone thing he just did. That's a big ten on the weirdo-meter!"

"It's just a trick. Big deal."

"If you think that's no big deal, you're a big ten on the weirdo-meter, too." She wrung her sponge, and brown water dripped into the bucket. "Yuck!"

I had already washed my set of windows and was now polishing out the streaks with newspaper, just how Dad had taught us at our old house. As I polished, I looked out onto the quiet neighborhood that would soon be ours. Across the street, an Asian kid about my age was walking a small dog that sniffed everything they passed. The boy was singing along with some song on his iPod. They passed an elderly black couple returning from the grocery store, each carrying one bag. The woman stopped to pet the dog and said something, and the boy and man both laughed.

"I'm starving," Ella complained. "This has to be cruel and unusual punishment."

"Listening to you whine all day is cruel and *usual* punishment."

"Hungry?" a voice boomed from the doorway. Ella and I both jumped.

Ella leaned toward me and whispered, "We need to put a bell around his neck. How'd he get to be so sneaky?"

"I prefer to think of it as moving through the world humbly," Mr. Mital said. "Only calling attention to yourself when you have something to contribute."

Ella quickly recovered her poise and threw her dirty sponge into the bucket. "You asked us if we're hungry, and we could use some food."

Mr. Mital smiled. "I do get distracted sometimes. Let's take a look at what we've got."

The kitchen looked like someone had driven a truck through it, then backed up to hit anything they'd missed the first time. The paint on the cabinets was chipped and peeling off. The stove had been pulled away from the wall, and all the tubes and wires and stuff at the back had been pulled off. There was one rickety chair, and it was piled with tools.

"There's no refrigerator," Ella said, her voice a little desperate. If she went too long between meals, things could get ugly. "Did you order pizza or Chinese or something?"

Mr. Mital opened the kitchen door, which led to a back porch. He bent over and dragged a large ice chest into the kitchen. "Got everything we need right here." He flipped open the lid of the ice chest and started tossing food backward over his shoulder without looking. Ella and I leaped up and began snatching things out of the air. Slices of bread, small bags of potato chips, individually wrapped slices of bologna, peaches, tiny packets of salt and pepper.

At first, for Ella and me to be hopping around the kitchen grabbing food out of the air was one more strange thing in a series of strange things that had happened since we met Mr. Mital. But then suddenly it was kind of fun, too. Ella was laughing and pirouetting like a ballet dancer as she caught a flying piece of bread. I pretended to be a pro baseball player, snagging a peach like a pop fly. I waved it around and made crowd-cheering noises.

Then Mr. Mital closed the lid, sat on it, and bit into a peach. He smiled at Ella. "You think my sleight of hand with the cell phones was weird, but there's a black man named Fred Jones who pulled off a magic trick that's even weirder. He made supermarkets appear when there hadn't been any. Forever changed the way America eats."

Mr. Mital pointed at my sandwich. "A black man named Joseph Lee affected how bread is made. Another black man named Lloyd Hall made sure that the bologna you're eating is safe. And a black man named George Crum invented potato chips." He gestured around the room. "This whole room is filled with a kind of magic that changed the world."

"Black magic," Ella said.

FREDERICK McKINLEY JONES

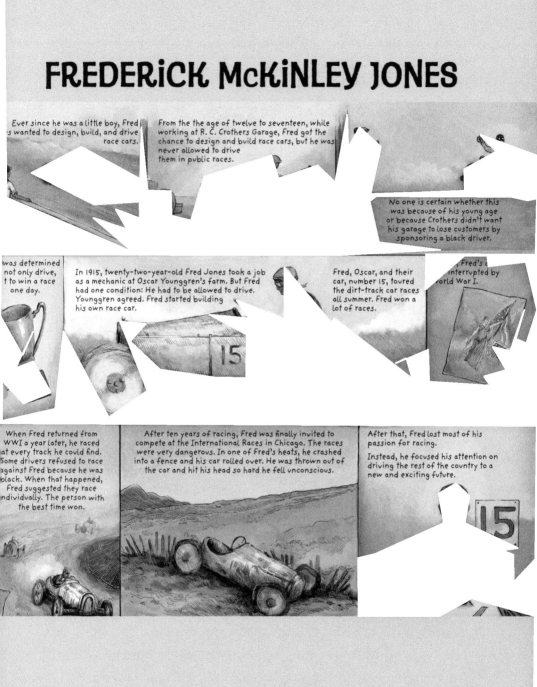

Ever since he was a little boy, Fred wanted to design, build, and drive race cars.

From the the age of twelve to seventeen, while working at R. C. Crothers Garage, Fred got the chance to design and build race cars, but he was never allowed to drive them in public races.

No one is certain whether this was because of his young age or because Crothers didn't want his garage to lose customers by sponsoring a black driver.

was determined not only drive, t to win a race one day.

In 1915, twenty-two-year-old Fred Jones took a job as a mechanic at Oscar Younggren's farm. But Fred had one condition: He had to be allowed to drive. Younggren agreed. Fred started building his own race car.

Fred, Oscar, and their car, number 15, toured the dirt-track car races all summer. Fred won a lot of races.

Fred's interrupted by World War I.

When Fred returned from WWI a year later, he raced at every track he could find. Some drivers refused to race against Fred because he was black. When that happened, Fred suggested they race individually. The person with the best time won.

After ten years of racing, Fred was finally invited to compete at the International Races in Chicago. The races were very dangerous. In one of Fred's heats, he crashed into a fence and his car rolled over. He was thrown out of the car and hit his head so hard he fell unconscious.

After that, Fred lost most of his passion for racing.

Instead, he focused his attention on driving the rest of the country to a new and exciting future.

FREDERICK McKINLEY JONES
AN INVENTIVE LIFE

Runaway

Frederick McKinley Jones was born in Covington, Kentucky, on May 17, 1893, and his African-American mother died when he was a toddler. Concerned that his son would not receive a proper education, his Irish-American father left eight-year-old Fred at Saint Mary's Catholic church in Cincinnati, Ohio. A year later, Fred's father died, leaving Fred an orphan.

The education that his father had hoped for ended at sixth grade, because at the age of twelve, Fred ran away from the church and took a job as a clean-up boy at the R.C. Crothers Garage. Here he became fascinated with learning how to design, build, and fix race cars.

At nineteen, Fred's restless nature and passion to learn took him on an adventure. He hopped a train to the South, but was discouraged by the racism and lack of employment he encountered there.

From Race Cars to Refrigerator Cars

In 1912, nineteen-year-old Jones took a job at an enormous farm in Hallock, Minnesota, where he was put in charge of maintaining all the mechanical and electrical equipment. In 1918, Jones enlisted to fight in World War I. He was assigned to an all-black unit and was shipped to France. With a crew of German prisoners, Jones was in charge of rewiring the electricity in several camps and keeping the telephone and telegraph systems working. He was an exceptional soldier, though he hated the idea of a segregated army.

When he was discharged in 1919, he returned to Hallock and made a living fixing anything mechanical and electrical for the townspeople.

One of Jones's jobs was to drive the local doctors around the countryside as they made house calls. When Jones saw how difficult it was for the doctors to get to their patients through the heavy snow of Minnesota's winters, he built a snowmobile out of an old airplane body and used the propeller to power it through the snow. Although Jones did not invent the snowmobile, he innovated and improved it over the next few years.

A few years later, in 1923, Jones again came to the doctors' rescue. Jones had been hired to install an X-ray machine in the Hallock hospital. However, it was harmful to keep moving patients from their beds to the X-ray room, so Jones invented a portable X-ray machine, which also took better X-rays than the other machine. As usual, Jones's reward was in solving the puzzle, not in turning a profit, so he never sought a patent.

Jones's big breakthrough came in 1927, when he was asked to help out the owners of a Hallock movie theater. Movies had just started to incorporate sound, with the dialogue and music recorded on phonograph records that had to be played while the film flashed on the screen. The equipment was expensive, and the owners of the theater thought maybe Jones could rig something cheaper. Using round blades from a plow, he again created a machine that was cheaper and better than the expensive factory equipment.

Soon word of mouth about the clever local inventor reached the ear of Joseph Numero, the owner of Ultraphone Sound Systems in Minneapolis, who offered Jones a job. Although it was difficult for Jones to leave Hallock and all his friends, he knew that he would never have an opportunity like this again.

The collaboration between Fred Jones and Joseph Numero continued for thirty years. Numero furnished Jones with an apartment above the shop, paid all his bills, and gave him a modest salary in exchange for owning the rights to whatever Jones developed. They shook hands, which was the only contract they ever had.

During those years together, Jones innovated all kinds of things, but it was his work on the first reliable refrigerated truck that transformed his life. It was so effective that Numero got out of the movie equipment business to focus on building more refrigerated trucks. These trucks were able to carry foods for thousands of miles without spoiling. Americans could therefore get more fresh foods at a cheaper price.

Numero's company, Thermo King, became number one in refrigerated trucks. Jones then invented the "Atmosphere Control" boxcar, a refrigerated railroad car. He tested it himself by riding over 250,000 miles in trains between 1948 and 1950. When his perfectionist side was finally satisfied, his invention was marketed, and again the world was about to change.

The Long Way Home

In 1923, while still living in Hallock, Fred married Minnie Hagstrom, a tall, blond Swedish-American. Interracial marriages were still rare, just as they had been in his father's time, and some of the locals were shocked and angered. But Jones had always been independent and didn't care what they thought. Unfortunately, he continued his long hours at work, which put a strain on the marriage until they soon divorced.

For the next twenty-two years, Jones continued his solitary ways. Then in 1945, at the age of fifty-two, he met thirty-one-year-old Louise Lucille Powell, a widow with a teenage son. They married a year later, with Jones determined not to make the same mistakes he'd made in his first marriage. He devoted himself to being a good father to his stepson, Tate. Unfortunately, only three months after the wedding, Tate died of leukemia.

By the 1950s, Jones's fame was increasing. Articles about his accomplishments began to appear in newspapers and magazines. He was invited to become the first African-American member of the American Society of Refrigeration Engineers. Howard University awarded him an honorary doctorate degree.

Fred Jones died of lung cancer on February 21, 1962; he was sixty-eight years old. Perhaps the most prestigious of his many honors was awarded after his death, in 1991, when President George W. Bush bestowed the National Medal of Technology on Jones and Numero. They were the first people in history to receive the honor posthumously and Jones was the first African American to receive the honor.

JOSEPH LEE
(1849–1905)
Bread Machine

ELLA'S FAST FACTS:

* The state of Kansas produces enough wheat annually to bake thirty-six billion loaves of bread.

* An acre of wheat can make enough bread to feed 9,000 people for an entire day.

Without JOSEPH LEE, we might never have had fried chicken. He didn't invent fried chicken. He didn't even invent the bread crumbs that coat fried chicken. What he did invent was the machine that makes bread and the machine that makes bread crumbs. Despite his humble

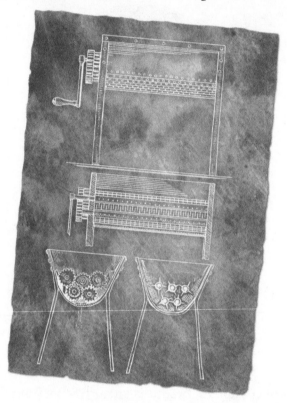

upbringing in Boston, he rose from his job as a bakery boy to become the owner of two successful restaurants, as well as a catering business for the wealthy, and the operator of a summer resort. In 1895, he patented the idea for a machine that would grind stale, otherwise unusable bread into crumbs to be used in cooking. After that, he invented a bread-making machine that made bread faster than six people could and more cheaply. Both machines are the basis for thousands of similar machines used around the world today.

LLOYD A. HALL
(1894–1971)
Food Preservation

ELLA'S FAST FACTS:

* Before 1860, people thought food spoiled suddenly, like turning on a light switch.

* French chemist Louis Pasteur (1822–1895) proved that microorganisms were behind food spoilage, which happened gradually as they grew and spread throughout the food.

Look, I know germs and microbes and all those other microscopic creatures have an important place in the whole ecosystem thing — I get that. But some of them are just plain creepy and disgusting and need to be exterminated! Fortunately, LLOYD HALL figured out a way to do just that. No, he's not the kind of exterminator that comes through the house and sprays termites. He's the guy who figured out how to keep our food from spoiling so that we can all eat fresher food at a reasonable cost. He figured out how to combine sodium chloride with crystals of sodium nitrate and nitrite, which kept the nitrogen in the air from spoiling food. His patented method is still used today to preserve meats. He also discovered that some of the spices (such as ginger and cloves) that people were using to preserve food contained molds and bacteria that actually made the food go bad faster. He invented a way to use ethylene oxide gas in a vacuum chamber to kill the evil microbes. Later, his method was adapted to sterilize prescription drugs, medical instruments, and cosmetics. So, thanks to Lloyd and his more than one hundred patents, we all eat a lot better — and safer.

GEORGE CRUM
(1822–1914)
Potato Chips

ELLA'S FAST FACTS:

* Potato chips use 10 percent of the U.S. potato crop.

* Potato chips are the most popular snack food in America.

* Worldwide, people spend $16.4 billion on potato chips every year.

Finally, something I really care about: potato chips! I couldn't survive one day of school lunch without those yummy chips to keep my taste buds alive. Thank you, GEORGE CRUM, for inventing them in 1853. Crum was a chef at a fancy hotel in Saratoga Springs, New York. Half black, half Huron Indian, he must have felt a little intimidated when, as the story goes, Cornelius Vanderbilt (one of the the wealthiest people in the United States), sent his meal back to the kitchen complaining that his potatoes were too soggy. Crum sliced the potatoes thinner and cooked them. But Vanderbilt sent them back again. Crum decided to teach the fussy moneybags a lesson: he sliced the potatoes as thin as coins and fried them in boiling oil. Now they were too crisp to be eaten with a fork (and the snobs back then wouldn't eat with their fingers). To Crum's surprise, Vanderbilt loved them, and they soon became so popular that they were sold throughout the country. Crum made enough money to open his own restaurant, which served his "Saratoga Chips" and catered to some of the wealthiest people in America.

« 4 »

"If you bump me one more time, I'll drown you in the toilet," Ella warned.

"Then move your big butt over and give me some room," I said.

"What did you say about my butt?" She spun around and pointed the disinfectant spray bottle at me.

I pointed my Windex bottle at her. We stared at each other like a couple of gunslingers. All we needed was a tumbleweed to roll by. And given the messy condition of this bathroom, I wouldn't be surprised if one did.

"How's it going in there?" Mr. Mital said, poking his head in the doorway.

We both jumped. I was starting to think that Ella's suggestion of attaching a bell to him was a good idea.

"There's plenty of mold," Ella said. "Maybe you've got a story about some black inventor who beat Louis Pasteur to discovering penicillin."

"Alexander Fleming discovered penicillin in 1928," I said. "He was Scottish and he won the Nobel Prize."

"Very good, Herbie," Mr. Mital said.

Ella stuck out her tongue at me.

"But just like with everything else, he stood on the shoulders of the people who came before him. John Tyndall makes reference to the same process in 1875. And in 1897, French physician Ernest Duchesne noticed that Arab stable boys deliberately kept their saddles in a damp, dark room to allow mold to grow on them. When he asked them why, they said that the mold healed the saddle sores on horses. Unfortunately for Dr. Duchesne, when he submitted those findings in a paper, he was rejected because he was only twenty-three years old."

"They rejected him because he was too young?" Ella protested. "Thousands of lives could have been saved!"

"Happens all the time. You're too young, you're too foreign, you're too black, you're too female. And we all pay for it."

Ella sighed. "Yeah, well, maybe when we're done cleaning toilets, we can learn more about *that* history."

"You can learn it right here," Mr. Mital said. He opened the medicine cabinet.

"It's empty," I said.

"True, there's nothing in it right now, but it's packed to overflowing with history. With the people who dedicated their lives to relieving the suffering of others."

I thought back to my history classes, trying to come up with the names of African-American scientists he might mention.

"Ever hear of cortisone?" Mr. Mital asked.

"Yeah," Ella said. "Grandma takes it for her arthritis. And Auntie Shinara takes it for allergies."

"And a lot of professional athletes get cortisone injections when they are injured," I added.

"They can all thank a black man, Dr. Percy Julian, for easing their pain. Also, the fourteen million people who get blood transfusions every year can thank a black doctor named Charles Drew. The 700,000 Americans who have open-heart surgery every year owe their lives, in part, to Dr. Daniel Hale Williams, who was a black doctor in Chicago and an early pioneer in the procedure." He stuck his hand into the empty medicine cabinet. "So, you see, the cabinet isn't empty at all. If you know what to look for."

"Kinda like a doctor examining a patient," Ella said.

Mr. Mital's smile widened. "Exactly right!"

I made a kissing-up face at Ella, but she was too pleased with herself to notice.

"What makes their accomplishments all the more remarkable is that they did it at a time when it was hard for a black scientist to be taken seriously. They had everything going against them—and they still kept trying."

I sat on the edge of the tub and opened my journal.

DANiEL HALE WiLLiAMS
(1856–1931)
Open-Heart Surgery

ELLA'S FAST FACTS:

* Open-heart surgery is when a patient's heart is opened and internal structures are operated on.

* About 694,000 open-heart surgeries were performed in 2006 in the U.S.

When Grandfather had heart surgery last year, I quickly
learned a whole lot more than I wanted to know about
heart surgery. But until Mr. Mital, I didn't know that
one of the first doctors to perform a successful open-
heart surgery was black! DANIEL HALE WILLIAMS
started out working as a barber and attending the
Classical Academy to study bass violin. There he met Dr.
Henry Palmer, a Civil War hero known as "the Fighting
Surgeon." I guess this was one of Mr. Mital's "shoulders
of giants," because Williams immediately dedicated himself
to becoming a surgeon. After becoming a doctor, he
became a "fighting surgeon" like Dr. Palmer by fighting
prejudice. Realizing that blacks had a hard time getting
into medical and nursing schools — or receiving good
medical care in hospitals — in 1891 Dr. Williams founded
Provident Hospital, Chicago's first nonsegregated
hospital, which also included a nursing school for African
Americans. In 1893, he was one of the first doctors to
perform open-heart surgery without losing the patient to
infection afterward (which is how most of those surgeries
ended back then). Dr. Williams also developed
antiseptic methods to prevent infection.

DR. CHARLES DREW
(1904–1950)
Blood Bank

ELLA'S FAST FACTS:

* The U.S. uses about 38,000 units of blood every day.
* Every two seconds, someone in the U. S. needs blood.

CHARLES DREW wasn't just one of the most brilliant students at his high school and college, he was also a star athlete. He graduated with honors from McGill University in Montreal, Canada, then went on to earn his doctor of medicine and master of surgery degrees there as well. He became the first African American to receive a doctor of medical science degree from Columbia University; it was there that he began to specialize in blood. Dr. Drew developed the concept of large-scale blood banks, which saved the lives of a ton of British soldiers and civilians during World War II. Dr. Drew protested against racial segregation regarding the use of blood (whites got "white" blood; blacks got "black" blood — how dumb is that?) because it lacked scientific basis, and he was fired because of it. Nevertheless, Dr. Drew was the first black surgeon to serve as an examiner on the American Board of Surgery. In Quebec, they even named a park after him.

At the age of forty-five, the man whose expertise was responsible for saving thousands of lives was killed in a car crash. Dr. Mordecai W. Johnson, former president of Howard University, said, "Here we have what rarely happens in history, a life which crowds into a handful of years significance so great, men will never forget it." I know I won't.

DR. PERCY LAVON JULIAN

Sir Isaac Newton said, "If I have seen further, it is only by standing on the shoulders of giants." That's how it was for Percy. His family always valued the importance of a good education.

Percy's grandfather, a former slave, had two of his fingers chopped off as punishment for learning to read and write.

His grandmother, who once picked 340 pounds of cotton in one day, worked and saved her whole life to send her son James to private school.

James, Percy's father, was a voracious reader who filled their house with books and loved to talk to his children about the things he read.

Percy told this story about something that happened at his college graduation.

"At commencement time, my great-grandmother bared her shoulders and showed me, for the first time, the deep scars that remained from a beating she had received during the waning days of the Civil War."

"She went through the Negro quarters and cried out, 'Get yourselves ready, children! The Yankees are coming. The Lord has heard our prayers.'"

"And then, proudly, she took my Phi Beta Kappa key in her hand and said, 'This is worth all the scars.'"

The shoulders Percy stood on were strong—strong enough to inspire a whole family into the freedom that an education brings.

THE MAN WHO WOULD BE A CHEMIST

Passion for Science

Born on April 11, 1899, in Birmingham, Alabama, Percy Lavon Julian knew at a very young age that he wanted to be a scientist. His parents, descended from slaves, encouraged his passion for learning. Percy's mother, Elizabeth, was a teacher. His father, James, was a railroad mail carrier and an avid reader of books about math, science, and philosophy. Both parents realized that a solid education was the only hope for their children's success.

Percy, the oldest child, was forced by segregation to attend a school with no science labs—unlike the whites-only schools nearby. His parents, however, accepted no excuses, and soon after his graduation from high school, Percy left home for DePauw University in Indiana, which accepted a few black students. The world was ready for a change, and he would help it change by being the first college-educated member of the Julian family.

Discrimination continued at DePauw, but Percy always heard his parents' voices encouraging him: "No excuses, son." He studied hard, worked many odd jobs, played in a jazz band, and helped out at the church. He graduated with many honors: he was valedictorian and a member of both the Sigma Xi and Phi Beta Kappa honor societies. As his class's most outstanding graduate, Percy was sure he would receive many offers from universities to continue his education. His white classmates received offers, but none came to him. He soon discovered that no one at the universities believed there was a place for a black chemist.

The Man Who Relieved Suffering

To be a chemist, Percy needed to earn his doctorate degree, but he was not accepted into any program. In 1921, Percy took a teaching job at a predominantly black school, Fisk University, in Tennessee. After two years at Fisk, he was awarded the Austin Fellowship in Chemistry at Harvard University. His academic achievement was outstanding: he earned his master's degree with straight As, but these were overlooked because of his skin color. Harvard declined to continue his teaching assistantship out of fear that white students would not want a black man as their teacher. Percy had to leave Harvard without the chance to earn his doctorate. He then taught at another predominantly black school, Howard University in Washington, D.C., until 1929. There he won a Rockefeller Foundation fellowship to study at the University of Vienna in Austria. Percy loved Europe. He worked with a demanding professor, Ernst Späth, to re-create chemical compounds previously found only in nature. Percy also enjoyed the freedom from much of the racism he had experienced. He had friends of many races and nationalities. He regularly attended the opera, went skiing, and played piano for his friends, introducing them to the lively spirituals he'd been raised on.

In 1931, he received his PhD from the University of Vienna, becoming the third African American to earn a doctorate in chemistry. He returned to DePauw University, where he was joined by a friend from Vienna, Dr. Josef Pikl. Together they worked to synthesize physo-stigmine (used to treat glaucoma, Alzheimer's disease, and other ailments), which they achieved in 1935.

Despite acclaim over Percy's achievement, DePauw refused to grant him a full-time teaching position because he was black. Tired of constant rejection by universities, Percy turned to private industry.

He received an offer to work for the Institute of Paper Chemistry in Appleton, Wisconsin. The offer was later withdrawn when the institute realized that Appleton was a "sundown town" and blacks were legally prohibited from spending the night there.

In 1936, Percy went to work for Glidden Paint Company as director of the Soya Product Division, which sought to develop uses for Glidden's vast soybean holdings. This division soon became Glidden's most profitable part of the company.

In the 1950s, Percy focused his research on the new "miracle drug," cortisone, which was derived from the adrenal glands of cattle. Cortisone reduced swelling, which alleviated pain from all kinds of afflictions and injuries. Unfortunately, the drug was expensive to create and few could afford it. But Percy developed a method of synthesizing cortisone from the soy plant, which made it cheaper and more widely available.

In 1953, Percy started his own company, Julian Laboratories, in Oak Park, Illinois. He then opened branches in Mexico and Guatemala, where he used the local yams to synthesize more products. He later sold his company for $2.3 million and worked as a consultant to major companies in the U.S. and abroad. In 1964, he founded Julian Research Institute.

Family Under Siege

Being a groundbreaker, Percy was naturally attracted to someone as courageous and ambitious as he was. That's why, in 1935, he married Anna Johnson, who went on to become the first African-American woman to earn a PhD in sociology from the University of Pennsylvania. It was fifty years before another black woman earned a doctorate in sociology at that school.

Racism and hate followed Percy. In late 1950, Percy and his family purchased a home in Oak Park, Illinois. A few months later, while the family was out of town, the house was bombed. The explosion took place outside the bedrooms of their two children, Percy Jr., ten, and Faith, six. This attack made the Julians dig in even deeper, and their neighbors rallied to support them, welcoming the family and condemning the attack.

Percy Julian died of liver cancer on April 19, 1975. His many honors included nineteen honorary doctorate degrees; his 1973 election to the National Academy of Sciences (where he was the second African-American scientist inducted from any field); a U.S. postage stamp honoring him in 1993; and in 1990, induction into the National Inventors Hall of Fame. But his real legacy was something that few others could claim: he reduced the pain and suffering of millions of people.

5

"You gotta serious case of the 'Bad Finger Boogie,'" Ella said, pointing at my hand. I was shaking out the numbness from writing so much in my journal.

"Too easy," I said. "'Bad Finger Boogie' is the original title of 'With a Little Help from My Friends.' They called it that because John Lennon had to use his middle finger when playing the piano due to an injury of his forefinger."

Ella shook her head. "You know, this game would be a lot more fun if you didn't always sound like a textbook."

"Don't challenge me to Beatles trivia if you can't handle getting whooped."

Ella laughed. "Oh, it's on now, loser."

"I'm not a loser, just a mocker."

"Ah ha! Ringo says that in the movie *A Hard Day's Night*. When they ask him if he's a Mod or a Rocker." Ella stuck her tongue out at me and laughed again. Then she did a little victory dance. Something had definitely changed with her. I could tell she was sort of enjoying herself.

Plus, Ella had been writing a lot, too. It was nice to see her interested in something for a change, even though she'd never let on that she cared. I could see a light in her eyes when she wrote, as if she was seeing possibilities in her own life she'd never considered before.

A bell jangled.

We turned to see Mr. Mital, who was holding a small bicycle bell, the kind on little kids' bikes. "You wanted some warning. I figured this would do the trick."

Ella smiled. "Yeah, that'll do."

"Well, Mr. Mital," I said, "it looks like we're about done here. Thanks for all your help—with the house *and* the history lessons."

"History lessons are all around you. Pick up any simple object and ask yourself, 'How did this get here?' and suddenly you're transported to other times. Like those traffic lights out there. Garrett Morgan once witnessed a terrible accident and asked himself, 'What if I made something to stop such tragedies?' So he created a type of traffic signal, and it saved a lot of lives. Not the first one, not the kind we use now, but one that saved many lives. Garrett Morgan also once ran into a poisonous mine to rescue trapped workers, wearing a safety hood he'd invented for firefighters."

"I don't think I could do something like that," I said. I expected some sarcastic comment from Ella, but all she said was a quiet "Me neither."

"What all these inventors and innovators have in common," Mr. Mital said, "is that they wanted to improve people's lives. I think especially for African Americans coming out of those harsh times when most of their people suffered repression and discrimination, they were inspired to alleviate some of that suffering. Sometimes in big ways, but sometimes in little ways." Mr. Mital reached into his pocket, pulled out a small pencil sharpener, and tossed it to me. "A black man named John Lee Love invented this. Didn't save any lives that I know of. But it sure changed the world as we know it."

I caught the sharpener and quickly sharpened my pencil so I could write in my journal.

Ella leaned forward and said, "What else do you see?"

Mr. Mital waved his arms around. "There's so much. Everything from those shoes you're wearing to the mailbox outside to the ice-cream scoop in the kitchen to the Super Soaker squirt gun. All invented or innovated by black men and women."

"Can you tell us about them?" I asked.

"Which ones?"

"All of them."

Mr. Mital looked at his watch. "Well . . ." He walked over to the closet and started rooting around inside. His voice was muffled a little as he spoke. "I suppose I can stay a little longer. But first, isn't there a Beatles song about a hole in the roof?"

"'Fixing a Hole,'" Ella and I said at the same time.

"Jinx," she said, "you owe me a Coke."

"And what happens if you don't fix that hole in the roof?" he asked from inside the closet. We could hear clattering as he moved around in there.

"Rain gets in?" Ella said with a shrug.

"Exactly!" Mr. Mital said. Suddenly he jumped out of the closet holding an enormous Super Soaker squirt gun. "And when it rains, it pours!" he said, grinning.

And he started firing. And in an instant we were soaked.

ALFRED L. CRALLE

(1866–1920)

Ice-Cream Scoop

ELLA'S FAST FACTS:

* Americans eat an average of 26.4 pounds of ice cream and other frozen dairy products per person every year.

* The most popular flavors are vanilla (29 percent), chocolate (8.9 percent), butter pecan (5.3 percent), and strawberry (5.3 percent).

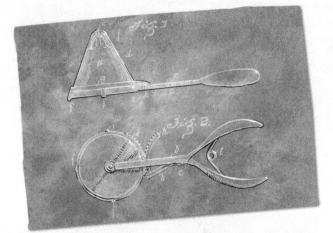

Inventing fancy electrical stuff is cool and all, but here's
an invention that speaks to my heart (and stomach!):
the ice-cream scoop. So simple you'd think that whoever
invented ice cream would have thought of it the very
next day. Yet it took a black hotel porter (that's the
guy who carries the guests' luggage) to come up with it.
ALFRED L. CRALLE was working in Pittsburgh when
he noticed how hard it was to dig frozen ice cream from
its containers. The poor slob doing the scooping usually
had to use both hands and a couple of utensils — and still
the ice cream would stick to everything. Cralle was thirty
years old in 1897, when he received his patent for the
mechanical "Ice Cream Mold and Disher," which is still
the same basic design used all over the world, more than a
hundred years later. We have one in our kitchen drawer!

LONNiE JOHNSON
(born 1949)
Super Soaker

ELLA'S FAST FACTS:

* More than 200 million Super Soakers were sold in its first ten years of production.

* Almost $1 billion worth of Super Soakers have been sold since 1992.

* In 2000, Lonnie Johnson was inducted into the National Inventors Hall of Fame.

Not every invention has to be something practical. Sometimes an invention can change the world by making it a whole lot more fun. That's what happened when a nuclear engineer named LONNIE JOHNSON created the Super Soaker in 1991. It would be hard to find a kid in America who hasn't played with one at least once!

Lonnie Johnson grew up in Mobile, Alabama, and went to Tuskegee University. When he's not designing the coolest squirt guns of all time, he's inventing other stuff, like the Johnson Thermoelectric Energy Conversion System, which is a system that provides a more efficient way to use heat to generate energy. Basically, this could be the hope for more widespread use of solar energy. Right now, solar energy systems only convert about 30 percent of solar energy into electricity, which makes it more expensive than burning oil or coal. But Lonnie's invention raises that efficiency rate to more than 60 percent. I know this invention is probably a lot more important than the squirt gun, but, hey, I'm a kid!

GARRETT MORGAN

Garrett Morgan was sound asleep when his phone rang on July 24, 1916, at 3:30 a.[...]

Under Lake Erie, thirty-two men were trapped in a tunnel filled with poisonous fumes. The fumes made it impossible for the rescuers to enter the tunnel.

Then someone remembered that Garrett Morgan, who lived in nearby Cleveland, Ohio, had invented something called a safety hood. The safety hood was a canvas helmet with two long tubes. One tube was for inhaling air and the other expelled the exhaled air. Both tubes hung to the ground below the smoke, where the air was cleanest.

Garrett and Frank set off into the tunnel with the only two other people who believed Garrett's invention would work.

So the police phoned Garrett Morgan. Garrett tossed some of his safety hoods into his car, picked up his brother Frank, and sped to the lake. He was in such a hurry, he didn't even put on shoes.

The men crawled on their hands an[d] until they came to an injured ma[n]. They carried him to the surface.

And then they descended into the tunnel again.

Garrett found another survivor. He hoisted him onto his shoulders and carried him out of the tunnel.

When bystanders finally realized the hoods worked, more put them on and rushed into the tunnel. They retrieved twenty-nine survivors. For a few minutes, Garrett Morgan and his brother were heroes. But the next day, newspaper reports didn't mention Frank or Garrett Morgan.

Garrett was disappointed but not surprised. He'd faced this kind of racism his entire life.

On that day in July, a lot of families had their fathers, husbands, sons, and brothers returned to them. Not only because of Garrett Morgan's cleverness as an inventor, but because of his courage as a man.

AN INVENTOR AND A HERO

Migrating North

Garrett Augustus Morgan was born near Paris, Kentucky, on March 4, 1877, the seventh of eleven children. His mother was the daughter of a minister; his father was a former slave whose own father was a white slave owner named John Hunt Morgan. During the Civil War, Garrett's grandfather J. H. Morgan joined the Confederate army and was killed by Union soldiers. Morgan's death freed Garrett's family from slavery. Twelve years later, Garrett was born.

Garrett's parents were sharecroppers; they farmed land they didn't own and only kept a portion of the crop. It was a very hard life. Generally, children started working on the farm when they were five or six years old and went to school only a few months a year. When Garrett was fourteen, he had to make a choice: stay in Kentucky and work the land or try his luck in the North.

In 1891, Morgan found work as a handyman and continued his education by hiring a tutor to teach him proper English grammar.

When he turned eighteen, he moved to Cleveland, Ohio, with only ten cents in his pocket. He eventually found a job sweeping floors for five dollars a week in the garment district and later became a sewing machine adjuster for two companies that made women's clothing. Morgan quickly became known as the man who could fix any machine. He also created various parts for the sewing machines, making them faster and more efficient.

Commitment to Public Safety

In 1907, Morgan, now thirty years old, started his own business repairing and selling sewing machines. Two years later, he started a tailoring shop that had thirty-two employees. The company made clothing with the machines that Morgan built. Both businesses proved successful, and he got married, had children, bought his own home, and became the first African American in Cleveland to own an automobile. But that wasn't enough. He couldn't help but look around and see how to improve the world.

In 1912, Morgan patented his Morgan Safety Hood and Smoke Protector, which he designed to protect firefighters. His invention won several gold medals and was cheaper, lighter, and easier to use and wear than anything else on the market. Despite this, many fire companies refused to buy the device because a black man had invented it. To counter this prejudice, Morgan had a white friend pose as the inventor while Morgan posed as a Native American demonstrator of the hood.

SAFETY HOOD
(1912)
Designed for use
by firefighters

In 1916, an explosion in an underground tunnel under Lake Erie trapped thirty-two men. The rescue seemed impossible; several men died in their attempts, and no one else was willing to try again. Then Morgan was called in. He and his brother put on the hoods and led a party to save the men. When newspapers later reported the successful rescue, Morgan's safety hood was ordered by fire departments nationwide.

Another time, Morgan saw a horrific street accident, which led him to innovate a three-position traffic signal that helped prevent accidents, which he patented in 1923.

TRAFFIC SIGNAL
(1923)
Designed for
intersections of two
or more streets

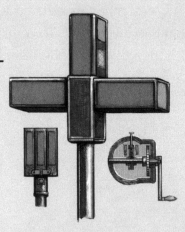

He also invented hair-care products, though quite by accident. While working on making sewing machine needles operate better, he experimented with various chemicals. He wiped one of these chemicals onto a rag and noticed that the curled threads of the rag had straightened. He called over his dog, a curly-coated Airedale, applied the chemical solution to its coat, and was amazed to see the dog's fur straighten. Then he put some on his own hair, and it too straightened. In 1913, Morgan founded the G. A. Morgan Hair Refining Company to market his hair-straightening cream, hair dye, hair oil, and various combs.

Devoted Husband and Father

Garrett was married briefly as a teenager and waited until he was thirty-one to marry again, this time to seamstress Mary Anne Hasek. Mary was white, and both their families opposed the marriage. Despite this, the marriage proved to be a happy and long one, lasting fifty-five years and producing three sons.

In 1943, Morgan was diagnosed with glaucoma, an eye disease that eventually led to ninety-percent blindness, but he continued to innovate, invent, and remain active in helping the black community. His contributions have been repeatedly honored by naming public places after him, including an elementary school in Chicago, a public school in Harlem, and a water treatment plant in Cleveland. Even the section of his hometown where he was born—Claysville—was renamed Garrett Morgan Place. And in 1991, he was inducted into the Ohio Science and Technology Hall of Fame.

Garrett Morgan died in 1963, at the age of eighty-six, leaving behind a family that loved him, a community that admired him, and a world greatly improved by him.

6

Ella and I were sitting on the front porch, soaking wet, when Mama pulled up to the curb.

"This crazy list had me driving all over town," she said as she got out of the car. "I had to go to half a dozen different stores."

"It's OK, Mama," Ella said.

Mama looked up at Ella. Then at me.

"Why are you two all wet? What broke?"

"Nothing broke," I said. "Mr. Mital squirted us with a Super Soaker. Did you know a black nuclear engineer named Lonnie Johnson invented the Super Soaker?"

"Or that a black woman named Alice Parker invented a heating system that can be controlled to heat individual rooms?" Ella said.

"Though the Romans first introduced central heating in 100 CE," I added.

"That's right." Ella nodded. "Tell her about John Lee Love."

"Let me guess," Mama said. "He was black?"

Ella and I nodded.

"There's more," Ella said. "Lots more. Our whole house is like a museum of all these cool discoveries by black scientists, only it's stuff we use every day."

"How did you learn all this? Did you come across some old magazine article while you were cleaning?"

"Mr. Mital told us. He knows all about that sort of stuff."

Mama stared at both of us for a moment.

"Where is Mr. Mital?" Mama asked.

"Inside," Ella and I said at once.

We followed Mama inside.

But when we went in, Mr. Mital was nowhere to be found. We called his name, searched the house, and even looked in the backyard. His tools were gone; his ice chest was gone. It was as if he'd never been there.

"That's kind of spooky," Ella said.

"Well, he did tell me he could only work today. That's why he suggested I have you two help him out."

"He suggested we come here today?" I said.

Mama nodded.

"Herbie, come here." Ella was sitting on the stairs beside my journal. Across the cardboard cover, which before had just said *composition,* someone — Mr. Mital? — had printed: *What Color Is My World?*

"Cool," said Ella.

I liked it, too. But I kept thinking about Mr. Mital. About his name. Something about his name. I pulled out my cell phone, typed in a name, and did a search. An article came up. With a photo. I stared.

"Ella, look at this," I whispered.

I held up the phone. Her mouth dropped open, too. "What the heck?"

"Roger Edward Mital. R. E. Mital. Spelled backward is . . ."

"Latimer," Ella said softly.

And we both stared at the photo of Lewis Latimer on my phone. Only the photo was also of Mr. Mital.

"OK," Ella said, her voice suddenly very scientific. "There has to be an explanation. He's like some great-great-great grandson or something."

"Yeah, that's probably it."

We looked at each other and knew that neither of us believed that, even though there was no way we could believe anything else.

Could we?

AUTHORS' NOTES

ONE MEASURE OF AMERICA'S GREATNESS is the enormity of its impact on the world through the thousands of inventions it has contributed. We have long been and continue to be a leader in scientific innovation. Unfortunately, many of the greatest American inventors have been ignored by history textbooks based on the color of their skin or their gender. Another measure of America's greatness is its willingness to right such wrongs, which is why I decided to write this book. By telling of their unsung but vital contributions, I hope to celebrate these overlooked role models so that we can all appreciate one another in meaningful ways.

I want to thank my cowriter, Raymond Obstfeld, for his steadfast commitment to the subject matter and his consistently good ideas. He is so much more than my right arm. I also want to thank my business manager, Deborah Morales, for her vision and contribution in helping me establish myself in the world of children's publishing. She has constantly encouraged me to expand my world beyond basketball, with very positive results. Lastly, I'd like to thank my editors, Karen Lotz and Katie Cunningham, for their valuable guidance and for giving me the opportunity to be a children's author in the Candlewick family.

—Kareem Abdul-Jabbar

THERE ARE TWO REASONS I WANTED TO co-author this book. First, the chance to work again with Kareem is like being chosen first for a pickup game of playground basketball. Kareem's passion for introducing kids to overlooked inventors is another example of his lifelong commitment to education and to community. As a teacher, I share that commitment with him. For both of us, history isn't a boring subject in school; it's the record of people's hopes, achievements, and even failures. Most important, it's a lesson to all children that the ideas that change society can come from anywhere—even from them. The second reason I became involved in this project is my son, Max, and daughter, Harper. They were always in my thoughts as I wrote. Their relentless curiosity and wicked sense of humor helped inspire the characters of Herbie and Ella.

Finally, it should be noted that inspiration produces ideas, but for those ideas to become a reality often requires a lot of help from our friends. Kareem and I did the research and writing, but Deborah Morales worked tirelessly with our wonderful editors, Karen Lotz and Katie Cunningham, on every detail to make sure the book turned out every bit as awesome as it did.

—Raymond Obstfeld

SOURCES & FURTHER INFORMATION

Books

Cefrey, Holly. *The Inventions of Granville Woods: The Railroad Telegraph System and the "Third Rail."* 19th Century American Inventors. New York: PowerKids, 2003.

Currie, Stephen. *African American Inventors.* Lucent Library of Black History. Detroit: Lucent Books, 2010.

Fouché, Rayvon. *Black Inventors in the Age of Segregation: Granville T. Woods, Lewis H. Latimer, and Shelby J. Davidson.* John Hopkins Studies in the History of Technology. Baltimore: Johns Hopkins University Press, 2003.

Hudson, Wade. *Book of Black Heroes: Scientists, Healers, and Inventors.* East Orange, NJ: Just Us Books, 2003.

Oluonye, Mary N. *Garrett Augustus Morgan: Businessman, Inventor, Good Citizen.* Bloomington, IN: AuthorHouse, 2008.

Rigby. *The Inventions of Granville Woods.* On Deck Reading Libraries. Boston: Houghton Mifflin Harcourt, 2002.

Salas, Laura P. *Charles Drew: Pioneer in Medicine.* Fact Finders: Biographies. Mankato, MN: Capstone, 2006.

Stille, Darlene R. *Percy Lavon Julian: Pioneering Chemist.* Signature Lives. Minneapolis: Compass Point, 2009.

Sullivan, Otha Richard. *African American Women Scientists and Inventors.* Black Stars, ed. Jim Haskins. Hoboken, NJ: Wiley, 2001.

Swanson, Gloria Borseth, and Margaret V. Ott. *I've Got an Idea! The Story of Frederick McKinley Jones.* Minneapolis: Lerner Publishing Group, 1994.

Taylor, Gaylia. *George Crum and the Saratoga Chip.* Illus. Frank Morrison. New York: Lee & Low Books, 2006.

Venezia, Mike. *Charles Drew: Doctor Who Got the World Pumped Up to Donate Blood.* Getting to Know the World's Greatest Inventors & Scientists. New York: Children's Press, 2009.

Venezia, Mike. *Daniel Hale Williams: Surgeon Who Opened Hearts and Minds.* Getting to Know the World's Greatest Inventors & Scientists. New York: Children's Press, 2010.

Videos

Kodama, Vicki. *From Dreams to Reality: A Tribute to Minority Inventors.* U.S. Patent and Trademark Office, 1986. VHS.

Lemelson Center for the Study of Invention and Innovation, The. *Lewis Latimer: Renaissance Man (1848–1928).* Smithsonian National Museum of American History. 2000. DVD. Accompanying educational material available online at http://invention.smithsonian.org/downloads/latimer_manual.pdf.

NOVA. *Percy Julian: Forgotten Genius.* 2007. DVD.

Websites

African-American Inventors. http://african-americaninventors.org/

The Black Inventor Online Museum. http://blackinventor.com/

Historical African American Inventors: The Faces of Science: African Americans in the Sciences. https://webfiles.uci.edu/mcbrown/display/historical_inventors.html

Saint Louis Public Library. "Inventions and Patents of African-Americans—19th Century." http://www.slpl.lib.mo.us/libsrc/inv19.htm

Saint Louis Public Library. "Inventions and Patents of African-Americans—20th Century." http://www.slpl.lib.mo.us/libsrc/inv20.htm

INDEX